Original title:
Sunshine on the Shores

Copyright © 2025 Creative Arts Management OÜ
All rights reserved.

Author: Wyatt Kensington
ISBN HARDBACK: 978-1-80581-685-0
ISBN PAPERBACK: 978-1-80581-212-8
ISBN EBOOK: 978-1-80581-685-0

A Floral Sunset on Reflections of Light

The waves are giggling, what a sight,
As sandcastles wobbly take their flight.
Crabs in tuxedos dance with flair,
With beach balls flying through the air.

Seagulls are squawking, with quite a tune,
They think they're stars, under the moon.
A flip-flop left, an adventure begun,
Who knew a beach could be so much fun?

Mermaids are truly just fish in disguise,
Wearing shells while they practice their lies.
Each starfish grins on the ocean's floor,
While jellyfish giggle with tales to explore.

So grab your hats, it's party time,
As we dance to the waves in perfect rhyme.
With laughter and joy, let's make it bright,
In this whimsical world of playful light.

Daylight's Charm on Sand and Foam

Seagulls dive for fries,
Kids build castles high,
Sunscreen slathered thick,
The crabs wave goodbye.

Umbrellas tilt and sway,
The beach ball takes flight,
A sandcastle crown breaks,
Oh, what a sight!

Gleaming Paths Along the Coastline

Flip-flops going pop,
A dog steals your hat,
The waves sing a tune,
As seaweed hugs back.

Buckets full of dreams,
Shells hidden in sand,
A picnic gone wild,
Ketchup in hand!

Enchantment of Waves in a Radiant Dance

Tides tickle my toes,
And laughter rings bright,
Seashells whisper tales,
Of krakens at night.

Surfboards tumble down,
Water guns do squirt,
A kite takes the stage,
In cotton candy shirt!

Celestial Hues Over Land and Sea

Sun hats on our heads,
The skies full of dreams,
Mayonnaise on sandwiches,
Life's better with screams.

Chasing ice cream trucks,
A bikini parade,
Chubby seagulls strut,
While we laugh and fade!

Illumination on Sandy Paths

The crabs are dancing with delight,
They scuttle fast in the warm sunlight.
With flip-flops flying, oh, what a sight,
I wish my dog would stop the fight.

A seagull swoops, a snack to nab,
While I chase after my lost slab.
My sandwich lands, it looks so drab,
Guess it's the fate of a beach-day blab.

Warm Embrace of Morning Light

The beach ball flies through morning air,
It hits a snoozer, who didn't care.
With sandy hair and quite the flair,
He wakes up shocked, life isn't fair.

The waves keep crashing, loud they roar,
But then they spill snacks on the shore.
With giggles echoing, we all adore,
The chaos made by the ocean's chore.

Dappled Light on Tidal Dreams

Kids build castles, tall and wide,
While parents sit and take a side.
A tide rolls in, the structures slide,
The frowns on faces, they can't abide.

A kite gets stuck in a palm tree,
While dogs go racing, wild and free.
We laugh it off, such glee to see,
In this mad chaos, life's a spree.

Glimmers on the Ocean's Edge

A jellyfish floats, oh what a tease,
It bounces by, it aims to please.
With splashes and laughter, the day's a breeze,
But watch your toes, or it may seize!

The ice cream melts, a sticky fate,
While we debate if it's worth the wait.
In the mirth of sun, we can relate,
To the joys that beach escapades create.

The Serene Glow of Ocean Whispers

A crab danced with rhythm, quite out of sync,
He shuffled and jiggled, causing a blink.
Seagulls would chuckle, a comedy show,
As waves laughed along, like they're in the know.

A flip-flop went flying, like a bird in flight,
Chasing a starfish, what a silly sight!
Sand castles crumbled, they burst with a grin,
As kids cried, 'Oh no!'—let the fun begin!

Luscious Landscapes Embraced by Light

A jellyfish wobbled—to grace or to fall?
With tentacles waving, it answered the call.
A picnic went wild, with ants in a race,
Stealing a sandwich, then gone without trace.

Kites snagged in palm trees, oh what a fuss!
A toddler cried loudly, 'That's all mine, us!'
Bikini tops slipping, causing quite a dash,
As laughter erupts, like a wide splash!

The Waking Song of Bright Waters

Dolphins were giggling, making waves cheer,
While fishermen moaned— "This catch isn't near!"
Beach balls went bouncing, a festive hoorah,
Falling on sun-tanners, oh, what a drama!

Children ran wild, with buckets in hand,
Building great fortresses, quite unplanned.
Buckets turned upside-down, dungeons of mud,
A treasure of laughter, a great sandy flood!

Soft Warmth of a Coastal Symphony

Sandy toes giggling, buried like treasure,
A seagull swooped down, oh, what a displeasure!
With a wink and a nod, the waves said, 'Surprise!'
As surfers fell over, to everyone's cries.

The ice cream truck jingled, a sugary cheer,
While matchbox cars zoomed, in pure summer gear.
Caught in the moment, as laughter defies,
The sun shone so brightly, oh how time flies!

The Brightness That Kisses the Coast

A slice of light smiles wide,
Waves giggle and dance with pride.
Seagulls wear shades, look so cool,
While crabs parade, playing the fool.

Buckets and shovels, they engage,
Building castles, turning the page.
The ocean's laughter, a joyous sound,
As flip-flops fly and fun abounds.

Illuminated Footprints in the Sand

Footprints sketch stories oh-so-funny,
Each step a dance, an ocean's punny.
Don't mind the jellyfish; they wave,
While kids trip over a sandcastle grave.

An errant seagull swoops for a fry,
As hot dogs roll and ketchup flies high.
Bikini blunders, oh what a sight,
Beach life's laughter ignites the night.

Sunlit Secrets by the Tides

Secrets hide under shells so fine,
Whispers of sandcastles built on a line.
A starfish grins, revealing its fate,
While a crab tries to imitate a graceful gait.

Splashing and laughing, the waves rejoice,
As sunscreen flies like an errant voice.
Each splash tells tales of comical woe,
In this wacky world of ebb and flow.

The Golden Horizon's Invitation

The horizon beckons with a cheeky grin,
Smiles abound where the day begins.
Surfboards spill stories as they glide,
While toasters toast in the sun's wild ride.

With ice cream cones that seem to melt,
We chase after joy, the warmth is felt.
As laughter erupts like the crashing waves,
It's a beach day, with antics to rave.

Fluid Gold on Tranquil Shores

Golden beams dance, a playful tease,
Seagulls squawk like they own the breeze.
Flip-flops flapping as kids run amok,
Even sandcastles dread the tide's knock.

A crab moonwalks, with claws held high,
While sunbathers giggle, not a care nigh.
Sunscreen squirt battles, laughter erupts,
As snacks get swiped by ducks who corrupt.

Cascades of Light Between Horizons

Light cascades down, like a wobbly slide,
Children laughing, not a frown to hide.
Kites soaring high with a tug and a pull,
While ice cream cones melt, oh what a lull!

Jellyfish jiggling, putting on a show,
They're the real stars, don't you know?
Sandy shoes squeak, a rhythmic delight,
As the ocean winks, what a silly sight!

The Warmth of Day on Nature's Canvas

The day paints laughter in colors so bright,
With sunhats like flowers, quite a funny sight.
Beach balls bouncing, in a wild parade,
While sunscreen warriors dance in the shade.

Waves tickle toes, what a splashy prank,
While giggles abound, not a moment to tank.
Seashells whisper secrets of the past,
As flip-flops fly fast, what fun to last!

Elegance in Waves of Light

Waves of light shimmer, with a hint of flair,
As beachgoers wiggle in their utmost care.
Sand slips through fingers, like a clumsy slide,
While dogs chase frisbees on a canine ride.

Sun hats fly off in a gusty giggle,
A dance of chaos, oh how they wiggle!
The tide tells tales of mischief and play,
As we bask in glee, in the light of the day.

Ethereal Gleams in Ocean's Breath

The seagulls prance, with such great flair,
They squawk and dive without a care.
A crab in a tux, so sharply dressed,
Pinches a toe; it's quite a jest!

Waves tickle toes on a carousel ride,
A dog in shades takes it all in stride.
With every splash, laughter resounds,
As sandcastles tumble to the ground!

Sol's Caress on Soft Sands

Flip-flops flapping, a dance goes wild,
The beach ball bounces like a happy child.
A sunhat flies off, caught in the breeze,
Chasing it down, while giggling with ease!

Sandy sandwiches, a twist of fate,
A seagull steals lunch—now isn't that great?
Grinning and grimy, we play all day,
While sunscreen turns us a peachy gray!

Blissful Glare Through Ocean Mist

Driftwood sculptures, what can they be?
A mermaid with feet or an old oak tree?
The tide rolls in, tickling our toes,
While a noodle fights back—who really knows?

A sandstorm bursts, oh what a scene,
A beach towel's lost in the air, so obscene!
With giggles and grins, we wade and we play,
As seaweed wraps 'round like a green bouquet!

Horizon's Embrace in Silver Hues

The sun's pulling pranks with a cheeky glare,
While sunscreen lathers like sweet summer air.
A clam's little song, so off-tune but bright,
Echoes of laughter from morning till night.

Kites dance above, in outrageous flight,
A picnic's in peril—oh, what a sight!
As we roll in the sand, a laughter parade,
Who knew that beaches could be this charade?

Radiant Play on Shells and Stones

Tiny crabs in their joyful dance,
Clinging to rocks, they take a chance.
Seagulls squawk with a comedic flair,
As waves tumble them without a care.

A sunhat flies, a flip-flop too,
While kids giggle at the ocean's view.
Sandcastles melt in the warm embrace,
As laughter lingers in this sunny place.

Light's Whisper Through Coastal Breeze

The tides are tickled by whispers strange,
Shells giggle softly, the sea's not deranged.
A beach ball flies, ricochets with glee,
Knocking over a sunbather's cup of tea.

Kites dive and swoop in a messy chase,
While seagulls express their sassy grace.
Children chase shadows, dodging the tide,
In this whimsical world where joy can't hide.

Joyous Glint of Morning's Arrival

Waking up to a day of cheer,
The beach is alive, oh what a sphere!
Surfboards wobble with reckless delight,
Chasing the waves, oh what a sight!

Flip-flops flop in a salsa of fun,
As dogs race the waves, they're on the run!
A picnic basket tips, spilling its charm,
And seagulls plot mischief, ready for harm.

Elysian Rays on Coastal Bliss

With laughter, the tide brings a playful game,
Who will be first to lose their name?
A broken umbrella, upside down on the sand,
Turns into a fort, oh isn't it grand?

Beach towels twist like windswept hats,
As sunbathers acquire some curious cats.
The ocean giggles and the sand makes jokes,
In this carnival scene where joy never chokes.

Laughter on the Breeze

Seagulls squawk in silly flight,
Chasing shadows, what a sight!
Kids are building castles wide,
While dogs run off with the tide.

Ice cream drips down little hands,
Sticky fingers, clever plans!
Footprints lead to nowhere fast,
Oh, summer days, how they blast!

Waves crash with a frothy cheer,
Splashing laughter far and near.
Here comes dad—he slips and falls,
In his shorts, he makes a call!

With a giggle and a grin,
Friends all cheer, let's dive in!
Life is rich with silly fun,
Where everyone is number one!

Illumination at Water's Edge

The sun pops up like a toast,
Watch out for the morning boast!
Flip-flops flying, off they go,
Chasing crabs, oh what a show!

Fishermen tell fishy tales,
While mermaids hide in their sails.
Sunscreen goes on, a sticky mess,
Who knew fun could be such stress?

Sandy toes and laughing shrieks,
Echo under tan-lined cheeks.
A wave rolls in, what's the plan?
Jump in quick—oh, where's the man?

Bright beach towels, vibrant scenes,
Tickling sand like clever beans.
With every splash, a silly cheer,
Summer vibes, the best of year!

Gilded Ripples of Joy

Ripples dance like little kids,
Splashing about without grids.
Sun hats on, cups of cold drink,
As we laugh, the dolphins wink.

Boys chase driftwood, bold and fast,
While old folks nap, the die is cast.
Who can say, 'What's that noise?'
Oh, just our raucous beach toys!

Kites soar up to paint the sky,
While beach balls seem to fly by.
Every wave, a chuckle waits,
In this place of sand and mates.

Laughter bounces on the shore,
"Whose turn?"—we play and explore.
With sun-kissed cheeks, we live this way,
In gilded joy, we surely play!

Serenity Singed by Sunlight

Chill by the waves on this hot day,
Sipping soda, all's at play.
Umbrella dance, a wobbly shade,
Sun hats flying, it's a charade!

The sand gets tangled in our toes,
Tangled tales, who knows what goes?
Grandma spills her drink, oh dear,
But laughter's the toast of the year!

With every splash, we squeal and shout,
Giggling kids run all about.
A crab sneaks by with a funny gait,
Making us laugh, we can't wait!

Evenings fall, the stars take place,
Flickering lights all over the space.
With memories bright, we bounce anew,
This joyful path is painted blue!

Morning's Caress on the Beach

Waves giggle as they crash,
Seagulls dance like they're rash.
A crab in a tiny hat,
Thinking he's the world's aristocrat.

Flip-flops slap like silly clowns,
Sandcastles built in goofy crowns.
A kid with a bucket and a frown,
Turns into a king, then falls down!

The sun peeks in with a grin,
Say hello to those who swim.
Everyone's laughing, oh what a sight,
Chasing shadows, oh what a flight!

Ears pop from the salt and spray,
Mermaids barking in their play.
A dog runs past with a stick,
Who knew the beach could be so quick?

A Tapestry of Light and Shore

Umbrellas bloom like flowers bright,
Sand sculptures wobbly in the light.
Flip-flops squeak on sandy trails,
Fish wearing glasses, oh how it pales!

Kids with buckets, oh what a thrill,
Digging for treasures, what a skill!
The sun's golden rays tease the tide,
While crabs in a conga line swiftly glide.

Beach balls bounce like a band on rent,
Splashing water turns to merriment.
A seagull snatches a sandwich in flight,
Leaving picnickers in a brief fright!

With every laugh, the shores unite,
Grinning grannies, what a sight!
Sand between toes, giggles abound,
What a way to spend time, I've found!

Warm Glow on Ocean's Canvas

The horizon sings in oranges and pinks,
While dolphins leap, oh how it winks!
A surfer stumbles, takes a spill,
Turns it into a clownish thrill.

Sunbathers recline, applying cream,
While jellyfish float, like a bad dream.
Tanning bears, no need for a cage,
And seagulls practicing their stage.

Children chase the waves with glee,
One's hat flies off, oh dear me!
A sandy snack, oh what a feat,
Finding it stuck to a wig's seat!

As the tide rolls in and wants a kiss,
A mermaid winks and says, "Bliss!"
With laughter echoing all around,
Joy and fun in the air abound!

Radiant Days by the Waters' Dance

Colors shimmer, the day is bright,
Silly kittens in a sunbeam fight.
A hammock sways, caught in its dream,
While ice cream melts, oh what a theme!

Frolicking toddlers, what a sight,
Splashing water, oh pure delight!
A flamingo floatie, the king of the sea,
With all the ducks saying, "Look at me!"

Pigeon picnics, crumbs everywhere,
And one that tries to comb his hair!
With each wave, there's giggles galore,
As laughter dances from shore to shore.

Sand in sandwiches, oh what a treat,
Turning our lunch into a messy feat.
As the sun winks down, we know it's true,
Every day on the beach feels brand new!

Shimmering Beams Upon the Surf

Waves giggle, they splash and creep,
Seagulls squawk, their secrets deep.
A crab in sunglasses strolls the line,
It trips on sand, claims it's just fine.

Coconut drinks, umbrellas tall,
Beachballs bouncing, wait for the fall.
Fishermen argue who caught a whale,
But all they found was a soggy tail.

Children's laughter rolls like the tide,
Kites in the air, oh what a ride!
Flip-flops flying, fashion in plight,
Even the jellyfish dance with delight.

On this shore, all worries fade,
Shells giggle, as pranks are laid.
With sunscreen smudged across the nose,
We're all just clowns, I suppose.

The Golden Hour's Coastal Ballet

Crabs tiptoe, a waltz so sly,
Sunset's glow, it winks with a sigh.
Pelicans practice their dive so grand,
But flops and splashes go as planned.

Shadows stretch like a cat's lazy yawn,
While ice cream drips at the break of dawn.
Surfboards wobble, a dance of their own,
The sea rolls laughter, it's happily thrown.

Sandcastle dreams with turrets awry,
A sand sculptor's plan—oh, my oh my!
Seashells and giggles, the treasures herein,
Among all this chaos, who needs to win?

As dusk falls, the fireflies hum,
In the distance, float the sounds of a drum.
With all this mayhem, what can I say?
Life's better at the beach in a funny way.

Luminous Horizons in Gentle Tides

A dolphin leaps, it's got a flair,
Trying to impress, it splashes air.
Tanned folks stretch like lazy cats,
While seagulls plot their food attacks.

Sandy toes and sunburned nose,
Laughter bursts where the wild wind blows.
A treasure hunt for the best flip-flop,
But who'll find it? Oh, what a flop!

Fried fish sizzling, the grill's a show,
Surfboards clatter, where did they go?
We chase our hopes on frothy rides,
But mostly we just enjoy the tides.

Even the moon can't hide its grin,
As we stumble 'round, with sand on our skin.
Tonight we'll star-gaze, oh what a treat,
In this joyful chaos, life is sweet.

A Tapestry of Light and Sea

Laughter rings where the gulls prepare,
A leisurely breeze ruffles our hair.
Beach towels spread like colorful flags,
While awkward sunbathers take off their rags.

The waves tickle toes, a gentle tease,
Funny faces made as we freeze.
A sunburned lobster waves with cheer,
Just another day, let's grab a beer.

Air mattresses float, take us away,
Paddles are wielded in a funny display.
Our beach ball bounces and flies so high,
But it's off to a stranger; we bid it goodbye.

As the stars outshine the day's fuss,
We sit in a circle, talking to us.
With every chuckle, the night still seems,
Like a silly movie, crafted from dreams.

Uplifted Spirits Beneath a Starlit Glow

The moon's a giant disco ball,
Glistening over the sand,
We dance like quirky seagulls,
With ice cream cones in hand.

Tiny crabs play tag at night,
As waves laugh and retreat,
We stomp and slip in sheer delight,
In flip-flops on our feet.

The breeze tells jokes, it seems alive,
While dolphins do their flips,
We sip our drinks with silly straws,
And drizzle laughter on our lips.

Stars wink at all our silly moves,
As sandcastles grow tall,
Our spirits soar like kites above,
We're having a ball!

Brilliant Hues on Serene Shores

The sun wears shades, a funky sight,
In colors fierce and bright,
Flip-flops squeak like cheerful friends,
As tides come in with delight.

Sandcastles lean, a funny plight,
As the tide begins to creep,
We scream, we run, it's quite the fight,
'Flee, or our towers fall, deep!'

A dolphin does a goofy spin,
It's auditioning for a show,
While kids on boogie boards fall in,
Splashing laughter, row by row.

With buckets full of silly dreams,
And sunscreen on our face,
We dive into the glittering sea,
In this whimsical, warm embrace!

Waters Reflecting a Golden Dream

The ocean sparkles, oh so clear,
Like soda in a glass,
We paddle cheerfully with cheer,
As wave might make us pass.

Our picnic spreads a comical scene,
With sandwiches not aligned,
Seagulls eye our chips like thieves,
Perhaps all snacks are blind!

We ride the waves, with squeals and shouts,
'This one is all mine!'
But as we fall, we burst with laughs,
Gravity's a friend, divine.

The surfboards flip; we tumble down,
Like clowns in a big top show,
Embracing all the splashes made,
In a golden sunset glow!

Radiant Melodies on the Beach

A ukulele strums a merry tune,
As beachballs fly about,
We dance like jellyfish in bloom,
With laughter all throughout.

Shells become our instruments,
With crabs that tap and sway,
While waves provide a perfect beat,
For our seaside cabaret.

Ballet on the sand, we twirl,
With sunscreen, hair a mess,
Our laughter echoes near and far,
As we conquer the wild, no less.

The sun dips low, our antics high,
A moment set for glee,
In radiant tunes on golden sands,
Forever young, we'll be!

Rays of Hope in Coastal Air

The seagulls squawk a silly tune,
As crabs do the cha-cha by the dune.
With beach balls bouncing, laughter flies,
And sunscreen's on, oh such a guise!

The waves are sneaky, splash and play,
I thought I'd dry myself today.
But every time I turn my back,
A wave attacks, oh what a knack!

Sandcastles built with thoughts of pride,
Come crashing down in rising tide.
"Oh look, a mermaid!" I'll declare,
Just in time for my old flip-flair!

The sun's a joker, plays all day,
While ice cream melts in disarray.
With giggles ringing 'round the shore,
Who needs a plan when you want more?

Harmony at the Water's Edge

A crab sings opera, loud and proud,
While dolphins dance, they draw a crowd.
Flip-flops fly amid the fun,
Who knew that beach days weighed a ton?

Umbrellas swirl like quirky hats,
Where sand gets stuck on chubby cats.
Picnics spread with ants in tow,
"Was that your sandwich?" "No, who'd know?"

Seagulls steal my fries with flair,
While sun-tanned kids just sit and stare.
The sun's a painter, strokes of cheer,
Turns beach shade blue to golden beer!

With friends all laughing, life is grand,
As surfboards ride upon the sand.
In salty air, we find our groove,
In this crazy dance, we twirl and move!

Radiance Over Waves

In waters bright, a fishy winks,
While kiddos splash and trade their drinks.
A sandy dog gives chase to waves,
While soaking wet, my towel saves.

The sun's a painter with a grin,
Catching freckles on my chin.
But watch your snacks, they'll disappear,
The seagulls plot—I live in fear!

Beach towels battle in the breeze,
While umbrellas bend like trees.
A funny friend with shades too wide,
Says "This is fashion!" with great pride.

As laughter dances on the sand,
We chase the tide, take life by hand.
With every wave, a new surprise,
Oh how the beach makes spirits rise!

Golden Kisses from the Horizon

With golden glitter on my nose,
I trip and stumble, spill my clothes.
The sand's a thief, it loves to cling,
To flip-flops and each silly thing!

A sunburnt lobster strolls on by,
While dolphins leap and seagulls cry.
The ocean hums a quirky tune,
That makes me wanna dance and swoon!

With each big wave, my troubles fade,
Where laughter blooms, the price is paid.
The beachcomber, an artist grand,
Makes castles high with shell and sand.

With friends aplenty and snacks galore,
We're kings and queens forever more.
As twilight whispers, day's end near,
We treasure moments, full of cheer!

Vibrant Mornings by the Waterside

Waves giggle as they dance,
Seagulls squawk and take a chance.
Buckets loaded, kids in tow,
A crab wears sunglasses for the show.

Coffee spills on sandy mats,
A dog tries to chase the splats.
Laughter bubbles like the tide,
While a toddler takes a slippery ride.

Sandcastles won't stop their rise,
Until a wave claims its surprise.
Shovels poke at stubborn shells,
As laughter lingers, in our spells.

The sun creeps in, a golden tease,
Turns flip-flops into a slippery breeze.
With every splash, we can't refrain,
From laughing at this playful gain.

Shining Moments Captured in Time

Photos snapped with silly grins,
As saltwater takes over skin.
Pictures of friends, all in a bunch,
One's lost his lunch while gaining a crunch.

Bright beach balls bounce with glee,
Chasing each other, can't catch me!
A towel flips, a drink takes flight,
And the beach is still a pure delight.

Shells are treasures, or so they boast,
Yet one's inhabited by a picturing ghost.
Finding folks stuck in chairs too tight,
As chairs collapse under their funny plight.

As shadows stretch and laughter fades,
We reminisce on the splashtastic raids.
Encircled by joy, we hold on tight,
To memories sealed in sunlit light.

Light and Water's Poetic Journey

In the morning glow, we stomp and play,
With foam-covered feet at the end of the day.
A splash battle starts, and chaos ensues,
While diving ducks just avoid our shoes.

Kites fly high, with tails that twirl,
But one gets caught in a lovely girl.
She screams and laughs, the kite takes flight,
With everyone waiting for the next surprise bite.

Sand is thrown, and giggles erupt,
An ice cream scoop takes a big hiccup.
Melting fast and dribbling down,
And a sticky puppy's still wearing his crown.

Time runs wild, like the surf on the shore,
Where laughter echoes and spirits soar.
With every wave, we find our cheer,
In this crazy, joyful atmosphere.

Embrace of the Radiant Waves

Floppy hats and flip-flops loud,
As we parade proudly, a wacky crowd.
With every step, we spill our drink,
While fishy jokes make us all think.

Towels tangled, who wears it best?
A sunburnt lobster poses for the jest.
Sand in shoes but we don't care,
The warmth tickles, a sun-kissed flare.

Darts of joy thrown through the mist,
We dodge them happily, we can't resist.
The ocean roars, a playful tease,
While we munch on dry land's grilled cheese.

As the day slips from bright to pale,
We wave goodbye; it was a sail.
In our hearts, these moments hold,
The friendly tides and laughter bold.

Wake of Light Across Crystal Waters

A fish jumped high, in a funny twist,
It wore a hat, oh, how could we miss!
A seagull laughed, and did a dive,
While crabs did a dance, feeling so alive.

The sunbeams wiggled on the beach,
As sandcastles begged for a moat they'd beseech.
Shells traded jokes, oh what a scene,
Making waves with laughter, so bright and keen.

Beach balls bounced in an endless race,
As kids in the sun made silly face.
Dolphins jumped, doing tricks galore,
While sunbathers snoozed, and began to snore!

The tides tickled toes, with playful intent,
In a world where time was joyfully spent.
Waves whispered secrets, oh, such delight,
In the wake of the day, everything felt right.

Daylight Serenade at Water's Edge

Crabs in sunglasses strutted with flair,
Stealing snacks from unsuspecting pairs.
A jellyfish jived, wearing a bow,
While flip-flops flopped, putting on a show.

Umbrellas bobbed like colorful hats,
As children giggled and chased after cats.
A sea turtle glided, slow as can be,
While gulls took selfies, posing with glee.

The ocean hummed a quirky tune,
As seashells danced beneath the moon.
Fish played tag in a shimmering spree,
While waves cheered them on, "Come, swim with me!"

With laughter and joy, the beach held its charm,
As crabs did a limbo, oh what a calm!
The sands filled with stories, oh so absurd,
In a lively serenade, nothing was unheard.

Bright Reflections on Nautical Dreams

A rubber duck sailed on a bubble of foam,
Making friends with a starfish, far from home.
With a wink and a quack, they shared some tea,
While dolphins played hopscotch, wild and free.

Seashells whispered tales of mermaids lost,
As crabs crafted sculptures, despite the cost.
A sunbather giggled, losing her hat,
Chasing it down as a seagull sat.

Waves rolled in like a comical troupe,
Each splash sending sand into the air, a scoop!
The sun wore shades, watching all the fun,
As laughter echoed, "Aren't we well done?"

In the tide's embrace, memories unfold,
Of sandy adventures and stories retold.
In this watery realm where joy reigns supreme,
We float on the surface of whimsical dreams.

Gilded Weaves of Sea and Sky

Fish in gold, like shimmered delight,
They twirled in circles, what a sight!
A crab sang opera, oh such a squawk,
While a whale beatboxed, giving a shock.

Starfish held parties, with snacks galore,
As jellybeans swam, sweet to explore.
The sun tickled waves, played peek-a-boo,
As kids raced along, covered in goo.

Bright kites above danced in the breeze,
While sandcastles giggled at passing bees.
The breeze told jokes, both soft and spry,
Tickling the are those who passed by.

Seagulls traded puns in a playful fight,
As treasures of laughter filled the daylight.
In the tapestry woven, so vivid and bold,
The beach painted joy in stories retold.

Beachside Reveries in Glorious Light

The seagulls squawk with glee,
Chasing chips from a dodgy knee.
Sun hats fly like kites,
As everyone dodges those funny sights.

Buckets of sand take shape,
A toddler's fortress turns to a drape.
Ice cream drips fiercely down,
What a fine and messy crown!

Tanned legs tell tales of fun,
In the race to catch the sun.
Flip-flops in a heated chase,
Could there be a sillier place?

Laughter echoes, waves reply,
As crabs dance and seagulls fly.
Beach balls burst in the fray,
Who knew sand could make such a play?

Reflections of Beauty on Aqua

The water splashes with delight,
As sunscreen tubes get quite the fight.
A dolphin jumps, what a scene,
While someone fries like a chicken queen.

Floaties flounder, bobbing high,
As kids giggle, pretending to fly.
Sunscreen slathered on with flair,
Palm trees shrugging at the care.

Someone's hat does a twisty dance,
A lobster's hue, not by chance.
With a cocktail in hand, all freeze,
As that seagull eyes our cheese!

Sun-soaked shoulders, sandy toes,
Look out! Here comes a wave that glows.
Grins shine brighter than the view,
In this wacky, watery hue.

Waves of Brilliance Against the Sky

The tide rolls in, a splashy shout,
Waves of laughter never doubt.
Surfboards wobble, then they fall,
As beachgoers bust a friendly squall.

Tanned arms reach for the sky,
Inflatable whales just pass by.
Silly songs float in the air,
As someone trips on their own chair.

Umbrellas dance in the breeze,
Covering sunburns with such ease.
Tanned clowns juggle fruity snacks,
As giggles fly and sunscreen cracks.

A lifeguard pretends to be cool,
While kids splash like they're in a pool.
The horizon smiles with a wink,
This shoreline's charm makes you think.

A Symphony of Light and Sea

A beach ball bounces, round and bright,
Chasing laughter into the night.
Flip-flops thud, a rhythmic beat,
While sandcastles find defeat.

Seagulls make a cheeky call,
As kids race, trying not to fall.
Silly hats wobble on heads,
While cold drinks spill on sunburned beds.

Picnics spread, a feast for all,
With sandwiches that rise and fall.
Kites dip low, the wind's embrace,
As waves applaud our silly race.

A sunset glows, the day's grand show,
As footprints dance, they come and go.
In this blurred, lovely spree,
We savor joy by land and sea.

Glimmers of Hope by the Ocean

Waves chuckle soft as they dance,
Seagulls swoop low, they take a chance.
Sandcastles lean, a bit lopsided,
Crabs hold court, their gossip abided.

Children giggle, their buckets in tow,
"Look at my catch!" yells a kid with a toe.
The tide laughs back, it's all in the game,
Saltwater kisses, who's really to blame?

Bright hats bob like jellyfish on the move,
The sun's bright glare makes everyone groove.
A surfboard's flip, a wetsuit's embrace,
Laughter erupts, but it's all in good grace.

Ice cream drips down, a cheeky delight,
As sand sticks to all in the sun's overwhelming light.
Flip-flops flip-flap, what a silly sound,
With each merry moment, pure joy is found.

The Horizon's Warm Whisper

A seagull snickers, it swipes my fries,
With sandy sandwiches, we roll our eyes.
The sun looks on with a cheeky grin,
As we dive for a beach ball, oh where to begin?

Towels spread wide like a colorful quilt,
Sunburns and laughter, oh, what a jilt!
A beach ball lands in a stranger's plate,
We all share a laugh, isn't life great?

The ice cream truck plays tunes so sweet,
Dancing to the rhythm, we move our feet.
A tumble, a splash, in a bucket of foam,
It's all a big party, yet feels like home.

With goofy hats and flip-flop flair,
We take silly selfies without a care.
As twilight descends, our spirits soar,
We pack up our giggles, who could ask for more?

Daybreak's Touch on Coastal Dreams

Morning breaks with a loud, joyful cheer,
The sand feels warm, summer is near.
Coffee spills as I trip on a shell,
Sea breeze giggles, all is well.

Flip-flops clash, it's a cacophony,
Dancing seagulls laugh, oh can't you see?
As I search for the best tan spot,
I find myself tangled in a beach plot.

With vibrant kites that swirl in delight,
Flying high, they reach for the light.
As the surf curls just to tease the shore,
We wade in, laughing, can't resist more.

As evening falls, we gather with cheer,
Our beach bonfire's warmth draws us near.
With stories so tall, hotter than flame,
The light of laughter calls us by name.

Echoes of Light Against the Sea

The tide plays tricks, the waves play tag,
With cocktails spilling in beachside swag.
A log sits idle, a throne of driftwood,
Where giggles and tales spread 'round as they should.

Footprints dance with the breeze in stride,
Chasing the sun with laughter as our guide.
A rogue wave crashes, soaking a shoe,
We burst into giggles, what else can we do?

Umbrellas bloom in flamboyant display,
Like magic mushrooms, they brighten our day.
The sun breaks through, a mischievous glance,
And sea-salt kisses spark a new romance.

As dusk hugs the horizon with a sigh,
And sandcastles bow to the night sky,
We'll take our laughs, carefully stored,
To return once more, with memories adored.

Radiance over the Waves

The seagull squawks in quite a tune,
While crabs do disco underneath the moon.
A dolphin flips, with style galore,
Splashing water, what a raucous score!

A sandy dog steals my ice cream cone,
Then digs a hole, like it's his own throne.
With beach balls bouncing, laughter will fly,
As fish come up to see what's awry!

The beach chair's a fortress, I must defend,
Against waves that come crashing with no end.
But I'll take a nap, with shades on my face,
And let the sun win this silly race!

So here's to rays playing tag on the sea,
Making everything bright, oh joyfully free!
With flip-flops flapping and giggles galore,
This beach day is one we all will adore!

Golden Embrace of the Tides

The sun greets us with a wink and a cheer,
While sandcastles wave, they know no fear.
A beach ball rolls, it's a sneaky sneak,
As toddlers shout, 'We're getting our peek!'

In shades of yellow they run and they play,
Tiny feet dancing in the sun's bright ray.
Grilled hot dogs sizzle, what a delight,
While crabs grab snacks without any fright.

Umbrellas flutter like flags in the breeze,
Kids chase the waves, with giggles and squeeze.
Sunscreen on noses, like clowns in a show,
"Don't touch my fries!" you can hear the crow!

From sunrise to sunset, we bask in warm glow,
With laughter erupting, the time flies, oh so!
Let's build more dreams before we say goodbye,
As the tide dips low, under the painted sky!

Light Dancing on the Shoreline

The surfboards wobble like kittens on skates,
While beachgoers gather for snack-sharing fates.
A seagull steals fries and then takes a dive,
As laughter erupts, oh, the beach feels alive!

A picnic unfolds with sandwiches stacked high,
While umbrellas tip over, oh my, oh my!
Kids run with joy, chasing waves as they crash,
As the jellyfish waltz, in a strange splashing dash.

The sun does a shimmy, it's quite a sight,
As sunbathers flip, getting the tan just right.
An octopus painted, joins here too,
With echoes of laughter and big splashes anew.

So let's toast to the laughter and play,
For the joy on the shoreline will never stray.
With a wink of the sun and the tide's fun embrace,
We'll dance in delight, at our sandy base!

Warmth on Sandy Stretch

With sun hats big and shades too cool,
We strut on the beach, it's the best kind of school.
Towels laid out like a game of charades,
With everyone laughing, a band of cascades!

Barefoot we race, with ice cream in hand,
While jellyfish jiggle, in a line on the sand.
Kites flutter high, doing twisty turns,
As the ocean sings soft, while the bonfire burns.

We build our castles with moats and with flair,
Searching for shells, catching sun-dusted air.
Soon we'll have sand in the car, that's a fact,
But beach days are treasures, and that's just a pact!

So here's to the sand, and the blue lovely sea,
Where laughter is magic, and everyone's free.
With warmth 'round us all, we'll savor our fun,
Until day turns to dusk, and our joy's well begun!

Vibrant Touch of Waterside Glow

Bubbles dance with glee in play,
As seagulls squawk and swoop all day.
A crab in shades walks quite a mile,
He struts around with perfect style.

Kids build castles, sand's a mess,
They laugh and shout, oh what a fest!
A dog runs in, a splash, a cheer,
Now everyone is soaked, oh dear!

Celestial Reflections and Sandy Dreams

Stars flicker down to tickle sand,
While folks are drawing in the band.
A jellyfish in flip-flops winks,
It twirls about, oh how it stinks!

Turtles glide as if they dance,
Their moves so cute, they take a chance.
A clam, all pink, sings off-key too,
The beach is alive with laughter's crew.

Harmony of Light Upon Coral Reefs

Fish in shades are having brunch,
Bubbles rise, and sharks just munch.
They joke and share their tales so loud,
As dolphins leap, they swell with pride.

A sea sponge wears a funky hat,
While octopuses chat and spat.
They wish to party in the light,
And sip on seaweed juice tonight.

Emotions in the Gold of Daytime

The sun, a joker, beams so bright,
While kids slip, fall—it's quite a sight.
Beach chairs flop, much to their doom,
And umbrellas play in silly bloom.

A piña colada spills with laughs,
As fish peek up from their green baths.
Joy wraps the shore like waves in flight,
All in good fun till the night!

Dappled Radiance in Coastal Dreams

On sandy paths where seagulls squawk,
I tripped on my flip-flops while trying to walk.
The sun flickered down with a cheeky grin,
As I stumbled and rolled like a barrel of gin.

My sunscreen failed, I turned bright like a crab,
While kids laughed and played, oh what a drab!
They built castles tall, I built a tall tan,
In the game of beach bum, I'm a very bad man.

The waves whispered secrets in the salty air,
My sandwich took flight, I chased it with flair.
The laughter of tides made me dance like a fool,
Who knew that the beach was a slapstick school?

So here I will stay, with my jokes and my book,
Where sand meets the sea with a playful look.
Each wave wipes my worries, til I'm light as a breeze,
In coastal daydreams, I do as I please.

Light's Embrace on Beachcomber's Path

Strolling the shore with my shades on tight,
I waved to a crab that danced in delight.
The sun bounced about, in a mischievous race,
While gulls overhead wore a curious face.

A starfish politely asked me for tea,
As the jellyfish giggled, quite pleased to be free.
I dropped my snack, it rolled like a ball,
And the tide laughed so hard, it threatened to fall.

The sand tickled my toes, making me squeal,
With each little wave washing up, what a deal.
I scribbled my dreams in the grains that would flow,
Only to find them washed out, oh no!

But here on the beach, mischief is gold,
With every odd moment, there's a story retold.
Euphoria dances as I twirl with the breeze,
Just a beach bum at heart, taking life with ease.

A Celestial Dance on the Dunes

The sun did a jig on the horizon's line,
While squishy seaweed took its time to shine.
My towel turned traitor, it flipped like a kite,
As I chased after snacks, oh what a sight!

The dunes sang a tune, no worries around,
As critters congratulated me for falling down.
A conch shell declared it the funniest show,
As my flip-flop flew off, like a crow on the go.

With each sandy tumble, I returned with a grin,
The beach was a playground, where laughter would win.
The ocean suggested a splash on the side,
And I leaped in delight on this chaotic ride.

So let's dance on the dunes with a whimsical glee,
This coast is a treasure, just wait and see.
In the quirky embrace of both sand and salt air,
I'm a fool on a journey, with no thoughts of care.

The Canvas of Light and Seafoam

A brush of warmth on the horizon's frame,
I painted my antics in this seaside game.
The waves rolled in, like a laugh at my feet,
As I fancied myself very graceful, quite sweet.

Yet stumbled I did, with an auditory splat,
Right into a bucket that sat with a rat.
It didn't seem pleased, as it scurried away,
While I waved and chuckled, just another beach day.

With laughter behind, and a splash in the air,
The beach ball flew high, my worries laid bare.
My sandwich could fly, take a break from its fate,
As gulls planned an heist—they'd simply wait.

So here's to the scenes, so funny and bright,
Where each goofy slip creates pure delight.
In this canvas of antics, I dance with wild glee,
In a world made of laughter, forever carefree.

www.ingramcontent.com/pod-product-compliance
Lightning Source LLC
Chambersburg PA
CBHW072134070526
44585CB00016B/1667